FREE AT 40

By Ruth
Bayang-Stoffel

CONTENTS

PREFACE

This book is especially for girls in their teens and women in their twenties and thirties. I hope to catch you young enough so there is time for you to be financially Free at 40. It breaks my heart to hear about women who have no clue how to handle money; who struggle financially or lose their homes after their husband dies because he "did all that money stuff"; single moms working two jobs or more to put food on the table and pay for child care; women working past retirement age because they can't afford not to.

I hope to catch you young so you can better the future, not just for yourself, but for the nation. In my ideal world, every woman is self-sufficient and in turn teaches her children to be self-sufficient, eliminating the need for social programs like Social Security, which are not sustainable over the long term.

This book is very much about personal responsibility. It is not a how-to-get-rich quick book. Becoming wealthy takes time and it is a choice. My message is not new or earth shattering. But perhaps hearing it from me will help you "get it." Remember when you were a kid and your parents would tell you something, but it never really stuck? Then another adult gave you the same message and you listened? I hope this book does the same for you. Thank you for picking this up.

CHAPTER 1
EGGS IN ONE
BASKET

I'm sure you've heard the saying: don't put all your eggs in one basket. So why do so many people do it?

This book is meant to empower you to get more than one basket and you'll soon know what I mean. It pains me to hear people I know and love, talking and joking, (or maybe not!) about what the stock market's doing. At the beginning of the Great Recession in 2008, as the world watched stocks tumble, people around me would say, "Looks like I'll have to work another x years before I can retire. My 401(k)'s been depleted." What a sad statement. Their 401(k), like most Americans, is their only nest-egg, their only retirement plan, their only basket.

Even sadder are those counting on Social Security to help them with their living expenses. A letter about Social Security, published on February 18, 2011 in the Dayton Daily News, reads:

"Yes, the greatest pyramid scheme ever is now on

the verge of collapse. The large working base that in the beginning contributed to only the elderly needy has now turned upside-down to the smallest point.

The smallest segment of working Americans will now be forced to support the largest group of aging Americans who are beginning to apply for the retirement promised by the federal government."

Many financial advisors say you'll need 70 to 80 percent of your pre-retirement income to maintain your standard of living during retirement. To me, that means I work my whole life in jobs I may or may not like. When I retire, I'm supposed to live on less than what I'm accustomed to? Does anyone else think that is just plain wrong? Sure, some expenses may go down. But not the cost of health care. That goes up as you get older. And what about all those vacations you're supposed to take when you retire? It's likely that the cost of fuel and airfare will continue to go up, therefore adding to expenses, not lowering them.

So I say: forget the traditional retirement plan. It sucks. How would you like to be Free at 40? Retired at 40, instead of 65, and have 100 percent or more of your pre-retirement income to enjoy for the rest of your life. How does that sound? By "retire," I mean be financially free. The number 40 is significant and relevant to me; I am in my thirties and 40 is a good goal. At 40, we are still relatively young, active, healthy, and vibrant enough to enjoy all that life has to offer. If you're in your twenties, you can work towards being Free at 30! Impossible you say? There was a time when it was "impossible" to land on the moon or for someone to climb Mount Everest. And then someone led the way and showed that it is possible.

Throughout this book, you will read true stories about average women who were able to achieve financial freedom by 40. I hope this book will inspire and empower you to do it too.

As of this writing, several states, including my home state of Washington, are proposing severe budget cuts, including cuts to higher education. At a protest in February 2011 in Olympia, a professor shared that some of his students came to his office crying because they didn't have money to finish the classes they needed to graduate. This professor was pleading with the legislature to cut spending elsewhere, not higher education, saying "our economic future is at stake." I fully agree with that professor's statement, but I disagree with the notion that a college degree secures your future. There is absolutely no guarantee that a college degree gets you a job that pays you a decent living. I challenge educators and everyone else to think beyond the traditional educational system, and look within for a better economic future.

If you are a college graduate and are on the career track, consider what else you may be putting in one basket. Your source of income. One job, i.e. one basket. What happens when you lose that job as millions of Americans did in the Great Recession? You lose your income too. To continue to provide for your family, you go out and get another job. Again putting all your eggs in one basket. What's to stop your new employer from laying off, downsizing, or firing you? Nothing. It's not something you can control. You can be the best employee, but even the best employees can be downsized when the economy takes a turn for the worse. For that matter, you can be let go for any reason if you are employed "at will," and most people are. Your employer can fire you for any reason as long as it's not an illegal one (race, age discrimination, etc.)

That doesn't mean that you don't look for a job if you're unemployed. Of course, it is your duty and responsibility to provide for your family. And yes, get a job. But at the same time, think about developing and creating a Plan B; a second, third, fourth basket, multiple streams of income. What can you start doing now to generate an income and secure your family's financial future, whether or not you get laid off or fired. A steady paycheck may seem "safe," but as we have all seen, there's no such thing as job security.

This is my definition of financial freedom: the freedom to work because you want to, not because you have to. The freedom to quit your job because you hate it, it no longer fulfills you, you hate your boss, it sucks the life out of you, it keeps you from your family, whatever. Multiple streams of incomes – baskets - are the only way to secure your own and your family's financial future.

During the Great Recession, the newly-unemployed looked to Washington, D.C. to fix their problems. Many were hopeful as President Obama rolled out his economic stimulus plan and promised millions of jobs. Let me be clear. This book is about personal responsibility and personal accountability. Your money is your business and your responsibility. No one else's. Not even the government's. It doesn't matter if you're Democrat, Republican, Libertarian, Independent, Green Partier or Tea Partier. Waiting for someone else to fix your life will not work. You have to fix your own life if you don't like it. Take care of your own finances and your own household. If everyone did that, including big corporations, there would be no need for government bailouts.

CHAPTER 1 RECAP: DON'T PUT ALL YOUR EGGS IN ONE BASKET; CREATE MORE BASKETS (PLAN B, C, D, ETC.) AND TAKE CONTROL OF YOUR LIFE.

CHAPTER 2
HOW MY JOURNEY BEGAN

Knowledge is power. Throughout history, there are incidents of books being burned to destroy knowledge or certain ideas. My own journey towards financial freedom began with a book. And if this is your first book on the topic, I am honored.

Before my journey began, I didn't think much about my financial future. I was making good money at a job I loved. I thought I would do it for the rest of my life. One day, a manager who I looked up to at work suggested that I attend a mid-career / retirement planning seminar the company was offering. He allowed me paid time away from my job to attend this seminar. That's when I first started to get a clue and when I first started thinking seriously about my financial future.

Not long after that, when I was in contract renewal negotiations with my boss, we were discussing pay raises and bonuses. I mentioned that I was in the process of buying a house and that a signing bonus would really help with closing costs. She exclaimed, "You're buying a house? That's great!" She went on to tell me that renting, especially for an extended period of time, was like throwing money away. I nodded, admitting that I had been throwing money away for many years. Then she shared that she had been very successful with some real estate investments. I had great respect and admiration for my boss and filed away what she told me in the back of my mind.

One Christmas, my son received a gift certificate to a bookstore so off we went to the store to find something to read. My son walked over to the Children's section and parked himself there. I wandered over to the Business and Personal Finance section, looking for an author I had heard on the radio promoting his book on eliminating debt. I couldn't find that book but stumbled on a different one that opened my eyes to the possibility of financial freedom. It was about investing in real estate. I remembered what my boss had told me several months earlier and was so enthralled with the book, I read half of it at the store and ended up finding a copy at the library and reading the rest of it very quickly. That's how my journey began.

There were so many new concepts I learned like passive, residual income - the key to achieving financial freedom. Put simply, most people earn active income. You go to work for eight hours, you get paid for eight hours. Rinse, repeat. You may have sick time or vacation, but that's limited. If you become seriously ill or disabled and you can't work, your active income stops. If you lose your job, your active income stops. On other hand, residual income continues, even if you're sick, disabled, or on vacation. You literally make money in your sleep. You work once but you continue to get paid over and over and over for a single piece of effort. Think recording artists and the royalties they get every time their song is played on the radio. How does one get passive, residual income? By acquiring or creating assets (real estate, businesses, intellectual property, etc.) that once is set up, will continue to pay you with little effort on your part. I did not know all this before picking up that book.

It's as if a whole new world opened up before me. Most of what we learn about money, we learn from our parents. I come from a regular, middle-class family. My father was a self-employed lawyer; my mother, an executive assistant at various companies. They both worked very hard to provide for me and my brother. Now and then, I was aware that we were behind on our household bills. My parents paid for piano lessons because I really wanted to learn it. But I was too afraid to ask for ballet lessons, which I really wanted as well, because I sensed that it would break the household piggy bank. My dad was the first in his family to graduate from college. He placed great importance on my education and mortgaged our home so I could get a quality education overseas. I know that took a huge financial strain on the family. My mom, who did not go to college, would reiterate to me the importance of a good education. She watched my grades like a hawk and pushed me to do better at school. I am so grateful for my parents' sacrifice. They absolutely thought it was the best path for me and moved heaven and earth to make it happen. But they didn't know any better.

While I agree getting good grades and graduating from college is important, it's not end of the world if you don't. Case in point: Bill Gates, the co-founder of Microsoft, philanthropist and one of the richest people in the world created something that pays him dividends over and over. And he's using all that money now to do good.

Both my children go to school, but I am also teaching them about financial education, which I first began to learn about in that book. Boosting your financial literacy and creating residual income is the best insurance against another downturn in the economy.

At the end of that book was information about a real-estate coaching program and a web site. I filled out a form online then got a phone call a few days later. This phone call, or so I thought at the time, was meant to filter me out and make sure I was serious about being coached. The person on the phone told me in no uncertain terms that the coaches were extremely busy and did not have time to waste on someone who was not serious about learning and doing. I answered all his questions in the hour-long interview and was accepted into the program. I know now that my answers didn't really matter. It was a way for me to "own" what I was about to enter into. To say out loud what my goals are and to have a witness to it. I enrolled in the program and paid the hefty tuition. My husband joined me a few days later in this new adventure.

CHAPTER 2 RECAP: PASSIVE, RESIDUAL

INCOME WILL SET YOU FREE. THINK ABOUT WAYS YOU CAN CREATE THAT INCOME.

CHAPTER 3
GET WITH THE
PROGRAM

To achieve financial freedom, you must get with the program. Do your own research and pick one. That program must teach you how to acquire or create assets. It could be a course on investing in real estate or stocks, or starting a business. Pick what interests you and go for it.

The real estate coaching program I signed up for in the previous chapter required attendance at a three day workshop out-of-state. That presented a conflict for me at my job. I knew there was no way I could get that time off. So I made a choice and called in sick. I have never regretted that decision.

The workshop was intense and gave you real life practice. It was exciting to meet people from all walks of life with the same goals and dreams. We all seemed to speak the same language. I came home energized. The program promised results in 90 days (if you did what you were supposed to do every day) or you got your tuition money back.

I followed the plan but at times it was difficult to do everything I was supposed to while juggling a job and family. I didn't enjoy making cold calls and dreaded waking up early on my days off from my job to put up real estate signs. It would have been more fun to sleep in or spend a lazy morning at home with a hot cup of tea and the newspaper. Like most people, I felt like quitting. It was then that I realized why the coaches recommended that we "get with the program" mentally. By reading books such as *Think and Grow Rich* by Napoleon Hill, and countless others (see recommended reading list at the end of this book), my mind stayed in a positive state and I was able to push through those "I want to quit" moments.

Books became a big part of my growth and expanding my mind. Who knew that changing your mindset can change your reality?

"What the mind can conceive and believe, the mind can achieve." ~ Napoleon Hill

Let's talk about mindset for a second. Be honest. When you saw the title of this book, Free at 40, did you think, "yea right!" If you think it's not possible, then it's not. But if you think it is, then it is. It really is that simple. Let me say it again. It. Is. Simple. Not easy. But it is simple.

Maybe you're 41 and you're thinking, "it's too late for me." No, it's not! You can still be free at 45 or 58 or 63. The number doesn't matter. 40, for me, is merely a goal. You can adjust your goal but it's important to have one and it's important to write it down because it makes it more real and keeps you accountable. More people reach their goals because they write them down. It's so simple, so just do it. Change your mindset from, "it's impossible" to "how can I make it possible." Get with the program. Positive thinking, self-improvement books (or audio books, CD's and DVD's if you prefer), may sound hokey to you, especially if you're new to them. But I urge you to keep an open mind. You are going to need all that inspirational material throughout your life to power you through the walls, both mental and physical. You must constantly choose to feed positive thoughts, not negative ones.

A Cherokee elder, teaching his children about life, told them,
"A fight is going on inside me. It is a terrible fight between two wolves.
One is evil. He is anger, envious, sorrow, regret, greed, arrogance, self-pity, guilty, resentment inferiority, lies, false pride, superiority, and ego."

He continued, "The other is good... he is joy, peace, love, hope, serenity, humility, kindness, benevolence, empathy, generosity, truth, compassion, and faith. The same fight is going on inside you too."

The children thought about it and after a minute one asked,
"Which wolf will win"
The elder replied, "The one you feed."

With positive thoughts fueling me and with the help of the weekly conference calls with coaches in the program, I landed my first real estate deal on day 89 of the program! One day left to spare! Throughout those 89 days, I had grown fond of one coach in particular. Juli once lived in Seattle, where I live, and became financially free at 40. Juli represented what was possible. She became my inspiration, my mentor, and my friend. You'll learn more about her in the next chapter.

So here are the details of my first real estate deal. I gained control of a home where the owner had quit her job and moved out of town to care for an elderly parent. She had no income and was in danger of falling behind on her mortgage. We ended up renting her home on a lease option; the renter paid higher-than-market rent in exchange for credit towards eventually buying the home. The future price of the home was set and agreed upon. I would get all the profit when it sold. I collected passive income for one year; it wasn't a big amount but I was so excited to be getting money from a source other than my job.

Due to some factors beyond my control, I had to short sale this home. That means the bank agreed to accept a lower amount than what was owed on the mortgage. But at the last minute, the financing fell through; the owner lost her home to foreclosure and the renter had to move out. We all agreed to part ways amicably and the renter got all the money he'd invested towards the eventual purchase of the home back.

At the time, I felt like I had failed. Then I realized I had learned so many lessons along the way. So many experiences I could not get from reading a book alone. I had learned by doing and getting out of my comfort zone. I got with the program. The greatest gift from that experience is the confidence in knowing that I can earn a passive stream of income. And that has always stayed with me. It kept me sane while so many around me freaked out when the economy went south.

CHAPTER 3 RECAP: THINK POSITIVE THEN GO OUT OF YOUR COMFORT ZONE TO PURSUE WHAT YOU WANT.

CHAPTER 4
THE MENTOR

Juli, the coach I first mentioned in the previous chapter, was moving back to Seattle. I was very excited and wondered if there was a way we could meet in person or even become friends. She cheered me on when I signed my first deal and jokingly said, "You owe me." I said, "Yes! When you're in town, I'll buy you dinner."

My opening came when I found out something about Juli from another student in the real estate program. That person told me Juli was involved in a network marketing company. This other student had tried to recruit me but I had zero interest. But now that I heard Juli was involved, I wanted to know more.

On a coaching call one day, I asked Juli if the information I received about her was true. She confirmed that it was and invited me to email her with my contact information so we chat after the call. I emailed her and could not contain my excitement when she called me on my personal cell phone. We had a long talk about the company and its product, and I was in!

I finally got to meet Juli in person weeks later, when she helped me launch my venture into the network marketing world. I was so impressed to meet a millionaire in person and thrilled to discover she was just as down-to-earth, warm, and genuine as she sounded on the phone.

Much like mine, Juli's path towards financial freedom began with a book. To quote Juli herself, Robert Kiyosaki's *Rich Dad, Poor Dad* "blew all her circuits" and opened up her eyes to the value of a residual income. Both of Juli's parents were educators and she too had a love of teaching. She was one step away from certification when she looked at the starting salary of a teacher and saw that she made more money waiting tables, part-time, while putting herself through college. She knew that that was not the life she wanted for herself.

Juli began investing in real estate and enrolled in the same coaching program I did. She often tells me that she used to be an introvert and her biggest fear was talking to people. The program requires that you call, meet, and yes, talk to sellers frequently and this forced her to go outside her comfort zone. Juli revealed that she was so nervous during her first few appointments, she'd call from her car just outside the appointment location to cancel.

The first deal Juli ever landed with the program is a property she still owns to this day. Since then, she has acquired homes and apartment complexes around the country that cash flow and provide her with a stream of passive, residual income.

At the beginning of her real estate investing education, Juli attended an exclusive wealth building summit which, she tells me, was a stretch for her financially to attend. She was a little apprehensive at first and afraid that the summit would turn out to be a bunch of rich people talking about all the toys they want to buy.

Juli was introduced and exposed to wealth-minded people, some of whom were already very wealthy. Everyone was looking for new and multiple income streams. And much to Juli's relief, they also wanted to find ways to help others.

Juli was soon able to quit a job she loved and buy a massage therapy business. But the business was a small business and one that required her to be present to generate an income. If she didn't show up, she didn't get paid. Much like a job. Except this time, she owned her job. Juli was looking for a different way to create residual income; one where she could leverage the skills and time of other people. Juli also wanted to find a way to help her friends become financially free. She told me, "The only thing bad about being retired at 40 is no one can play with you. I call up my friends and they either have to work or they have no money to play with me." Most of Juli's friends weren't interested in, or were intimidated by, investing in real estate, even if it meant they too could be financially free.

Juli had a regular client at her massage business whom she knew hadn't worked in years. During one appointment, the conversation turned to income. The client revealed that she got paid $20,000 a month and showed her a check to prove it. The client told her it was from a network marketing business she grew decades ago. The checks were still coming in with no effort on the client's part. Juli's interest was piqued.

Then Kathleen, a friend of Juli's, who also attended the wealth building summit mentioned earlier, called her about another network marketing business. It was what they call a "ground floor opportunity." Juli resisted for months because she wasn't sure about the product. Kathleen was finally able to persuade Juli to at least try it; she did and got amazing results. Juli began sharing it with her friends and soon her networking marketing business grew to the point where it was making more money than her real estate investments. Now she had a vehicle for her friends to become financially free that wasn't so intimidating. I, and they, climbed eagerly.

I was earning a steady, residual income around the time the panic of the Great Recession set in, at the same time people were fearful of losing their jobs and seeing the value of their 401(k)'s shrink.

Juli is living her dream life and traveling the world with the person she loves. She has the luxury of time and the passion to teach and mentor others to realize their own financial freedom.

CHAPTER 4 RECAP: FIND A MENTOR, SOMEONE WHO'S BEEN WHERE YOU ARE TODAY, AND IS WHERE YOU EVENTUALLY WANT TO BE.

JULI BUTLER has been teaching Vibrational Psychology, energy healing, and meditation since 1997. She has sought to empower people financially to impact the world globally and has helped hundreds of people achieve financial freedom within a spiritual paradigm. For more information, contact Juli at julimoosa@yahoo.com or find her at **abundancewarrior.com**.

CHAPTER 5
A PARADIGM SHIFT

I mentioned the importance of mindset briefly in Chapter 3. Changing negative thoughts to positive ones. The ones you feed are the ones that grow. Now think about your reality, your paradigm. How do you see the world? This is important because your perception of the world can limit you. And it may be time for a paradigm shift.

I want to scream every time I hear someone say "at least you have a job." This is what I hear: "The economy sucks, get over yourself and get used to it." I am not ungrateful for my job, even when I had one I no longer enjoyed. What I don't accept is the belief that "that's life."

The teachers in my son's school district went on strike around the time the Great Recession began. While some in the community supported them, others were quick to say, "at least they have a job." (Scream!) One man interviewed by a television station said the teachers should be happy with their salary, which average at $50,000 a year. He said, "I've never made $40,000 in my life, let alone

$50,000." This man appeared to be in his fifties and his reality was a salary of under $40,000 a year. He could not fathom making more money than that. It was beyond his paradigm and I felt sorry for him. I couldn't help but wonder why he had accepted that as his "lot" in life.

Let's look at multi-billionaire Oprah Winfrey. She was raised in poverty, but she did not accept that "that's the way it is." She didn't let that limit her. Oprah Winfrey was able to change her perception of the world, shift her paradigm, and in turn, increase her earning potential. You are capable of doing this too. It is as simple as making a choice to do so. There it is again. Simple. Not easy. But definitely not impossible.

How many people do you know who are in "dead end" jobs? Do you consider yourself to be in one? Ever see that old lady at the diner and wonder, how long has she been doing this? It's one thing if it was her lifelong dream to serve at a diner until the day she dies. It's quite another if she's there because she feels there's nothing else for her.

You don't have to accept your life the way it is if you don't like it. Shift your paradigm. Yes, you can go from the person receiving a pay check to the one signing it. You can choose to increase your income. All of this takes work. And it isn't going to happen overnight. But you can start laying the foundation right now.

First, you must fully accept that there is nothing wrong to have the desire to want more. Nothing wrong with wanting to be rich. And you wanting more doesn't mean that you're taking from someone else, that another person will have less as a result.

"A candle loses nothing by lighting another candle." -Father James Keller

Shift your paradigm from one of scarcity and poverty (there isn't enough for everyone) to one of abundance (there's plenty for everybody). The pie keeps growing, so everyone who wants a piece can have one. It is limitless.

I attended a workshop that Juli (Chapter 4) conducted to teach women how to "Get Rich, Do Good and Impact The World." There are two things that struck me most about this workshop. The majority of those who attended were in their fifties or older and had no clue about how to become financially free. That's why I want to catch you while you're still young! The other was witnessing the power of self-limiting beliefs; beliefs that have been held for so long, they become too difficult to shed, and it's easier to just stick with them. Remember, beliefs can be changed. But you must be willing to do so.

Juli said during this workshop, "Teach a man to read and he'll learn to read. Teach a woman to read and the whole village learns to read." This is not a knock against men. It's just the way it is. Women are naturally more inclined to share their knowledge. The workshop began with the question, "What would I do if time and money were no issue?" The answers were varied but all shared a common theme: helping others who are less fortunate in order   to   better   the   world   for   all.

As we delved into how one creates wealth, I sensed a heaviness in the room and I could see the walls in the women's minds start to come up with self-defeating   thoughts. One woman raised her hand and said she was disappointed. We had just discussed some of the ways to generate a passive, residual income and one of them was to start or create a business. She said, "I have no money." Juli tried to share how she had done it without money, but:

"A man convinced against his will is of the same opinion still."

You must be willing to shed your beliefs, your paradigms. You must be willing to see that those "beliefs" are really excuses. Eventually that woman's self-limiting belief caused her to get up and leave. She appeared to be disgusted, as if the workshop had been a waste of her time. I felt very sad for this woman. She was so set in her thinking that the ideas we were discussing seemed impossible to her. She could not let herself believe that it could happen for her.

The three-hour workshop was a first for most of the group, the first step in their journey towards financial freedom and building wealth. That one woman had chosen to quit in the first couple of hours of what can be a years-long journey. Like most things in life, building wealth and learning how to do it takes time. And it is a choice. You can choose to keep an open mind and soak in what someone is teaching you, or you can hold on to your beliefs and paradigms, some of which are self-limiting, and remain stuck.

I thought the most intriguing part of this workshop was an exercise where Juli asked us to finish sentences. Our responses revealed each of our paradigms and perceptions about money.

Here's one: **(Don't think about it. Write the first thing that comes to mind.)**

"Rich women are _____ ."

Here were some of the responses:
compromised, classist, philanthropists.

What was your response? Do you see how your response, if it has a negative connation, can limit you? This is a book about financial freedom, i.e. becoming rich. How can you possibly become rich if it means that you must compromise yourself or become a classist? Think about why you have these perceptions. You heard that message somewhere. Your parents? The media? What proof do you have that this is true? Do you think rich people are greedy? Why? Do a few greedy rich people make all rich people greedy?

On a radio show about money, a caller asked the host if she should help out a family member with money problems. The caller said she and her husband were willing to give some money and the host asked, "How much money do you have to give?" The caller hemmed and hawed. Getting impatient, the host asked, "Are you a millionaire?" Without hesitation, the caller said, "Oh no. We're regular, hardworking people."

Did you catch that?

That woman's belief was that millionaires aren't regular or hardworking. Having these perceptions doesn't make you a bad person. It's how you see the world. But you need to be aware of it, then change it. Only then can you shift your paradigm and grow, both mentally and financially.

CHAPTER 5 RECAP: BE MINDFUL OF YOUR THOUGHTS, THEN TAKE CONTROL OF THEM. ONLY THEN CAN YOU CHANGE YOUR LIFE.

CHAPTER 6
GET EDUCATED

"If you think education is expensive, try ignorance." ~ Derek Bok

This does not mean a college education. I have nothing against college. I, myself, am a college graduate. But some people think their education stops when they get out of school. Do not let that be your mistake.

Let me introduce you to Annie. She and I met in college and we are about the same age.

We lost touch after college but recently found each other on a social networking web site. While looking through her profile, I was impressed by what she had done since college. Here I was, still toiling away in a traditional job. She had the luxury of staying home with her kids and she was not employed. But she was, and still is, earning a residual income. She was financially free. And she had achieved that by her mid-thirties.

Her journey towards financial freedom began nearly ten years before mine. After graduating from college, Annie worked for three years in a traditional job. It was her intention to climb the corporate ladder, but she always knew in the back of her mind that she would never make as much money as the CEO or owner of the company.

So Annie and her husband, Zach, decided to open a business. Zach sold his car to start their first business. They did really well and with the money they earned, they quickly began to invest into stocks (without any knowledge or research) and other businesses. They put money into certain stocks because friends told them it was a good investment. Long story short, they lost tens of thousands of dollars.

Annie then came upon Robert Kiyosaki's book, *Rich Dad, Poor Dad*. Just like it did Juli and me, a light bulb came on in Annie's head and she realized the power of a residual income. At the time, Annie was living with her husband in her in-laws' house. The couple borrowed from his parents to invest in another business and ended up losing that money too. The in-laws didn't understand why Annie and Zach continued to pursue their dream of a residual income, why they didn't just sell their business and get "real jobs."

Annie told me at that point, they were hundreds of thousands of dollars in debt. But she was not willing to give up. She came across a notice for a seminar about money and personal development and decided to go for it, spending thousands of dollars more. She kept going despite her earlier failures.

"The desire to fail on the way to reaching a bigger goal is the untold secret of success." ~ Seth Godin

Annie's and Zach's breakthrough came three years into a network marketing company they had joined while earning a below-average income. After a total of seven failed businesses, today the couple has four successful ones, four "baskets" that pay them a very comfortable residual income every month. Today, they have also paid off all their debts. Annie is now in a position to give generously. She is the founder of LIFE Children Foundation, which aims to provide an education to every child. The purpose is to inspire, empower and free them. Find more information, go to **www.lifechildrenfoundation.org**.

The one thing that struck me about Annie is her willingness to get educated. As I pointed out in the beginning of this chapter, that doesn't mean going back to school to get your Master's Degree or getting job re-training. Get an education on bettering you, the whole person, and learn ways to create and maintain a residual income. Invest in bettering yourself for you, not for a company where you hope to get hired. Look into books, seminars, workshops, just like Annie and Juli did. That education will always pay dividends later, no matter how bleak it may seem right now. Yes, it may cost you thousands of dollars but remember the price of ignorance. Annie learned that first hand when she blindly invested in stocks.

Think about this. No one blinks an eye over going heavily into student loan (college) debt. And as you know, a college degree does not guarantee a good income. How many college graduates do you know who are saddled with student loan debt, scraping to get by. Some may have moved back in with their parents. Some are unemployed.

Hire a coach and/or mentor. Even professional athletes have trainers and coaches! You are never too old or too smart to learn something new. If you're not constantly learning, you are dying and obsolete. You must be teachable, no matter how much you know or think you know.

This reminds me of the story of the professor who seeks out a famous Zen master. While the master is serving tea, the professor talks about all the things he knows of Zen and its principles. The master keeps quiet and keeps pouring tea until it overflows the cup. But the Zen master doesn't stop. He keeps pouring and the tea keeps running out of the cup. Annoyed, the professor tells the Zen master to stop, because the cup can't possibly hold any more and the overflowing tea is just wasted. Only then the master replies, "You are like this cup. How can I teach you Zen if you do not empty your cup?"

Will you choose to empty your cup, keep an open mind and be open to learning new things? Realize that everything you do is a choice. Even doing nothing is a choice.

During my real estate investing, I would walk into homes about to be foreclosed and it would not be uncommon to see a fancy entertainment system in the living room and luxury cars in the driveway.

A series of poor choices made, in my opinion.

Another example: an acquaintance unemployed for months wondering how much longer she could make it on jobless benefits. Yet she was able to scrape money together for the latest iPhone, along with the data plan that came with it.

Don't buy that latest and greatest electronic gadget! Don't buy that car to impress the neighbors you hardly know and don't even like! Instead, use that money to better yourself, like paying for a seminar that will increase your financial literacy. Turn off the TV and read a book instead.

Don't spend your money. Invest it... in yourself.

Financial freedom is about being in control, putting you in the driver's seat of your life. Some people prefer a job where they don't have to think for themselves, don't have to take initiative or risks. It's okay if that's all you want for yourself. But realize that you've put yourself in a position of powerlessness. If you lose your job and have no income to fall back because you didn't cultivate other "baskets" or streams of income, realize that it was your choice all along. Hopefully, you don't have a family to support because you will have made that choice for them as well. You gave up control of your life and financial future in exchange for "security" and predictability.

One of my favorite quotes is from Robert Kiyosaki's

book, *Rich Dad's Prophecy*.

Kiyosaki writes:

"People who have the most security are those in prison – all their food, shelter, schedules, work is provided for them. But there is a reason we call them "maximum security" prisons. They have total security, but zero freedom."

It all comes down to choices.
What will you choose to do?

CHAPTER 6 RECAP: DECIDE ON A COURSE OF ACTION THEN LEARN AS MUCH AS YOU CAN ABOUT IT. DON'T BE AFRAID TO INVEST THAT MONEY. YOU ARE NOT SPENDING IT, BUT INVESTING IN THE BETTERMENT OF YOUR FINANCIAL FUTURE.

ANNIE LIM is a trainer of the world renowned program called Money & You®. She owns her own training and coaching company, *Living in Possibilities*. Her areas of specialty are entrepreneurship, parenting, health and well-being, and authentic leadership. Annie has owned and managed several companies in Malaysia. Her successes have been featured on Bloomberg Television and Malaysian prime time news. For more information, visit www.livinginpossibilities.com, or email Annie at annie@drannielim.com.

CHAPTER 7
MY TURNING POINT

I spent nearly twenty years in a traditional job as a broadcast news producer. At the beginning of my career, I dreamt about being the next Connie Chung (she was big back then and the only Asian I knew about). I dreamt about working for CNN or one of the big three (ABC, CBS, NBC) in New York, anchor the nightly news and travel the world, reporting on stories that would greatly impact society. One day, I decided being in front of the camera was not my thing and turned my attention to producing.

In the producer's chair, it was rewarding to see a newscast come together every night and know that I played a major role in it. I loved the power of putting words in someone else's mouth (i.e. the TV anchor). The first station I worked for ran credits at the end of the newscast and my name was the first one to come up - very cool for a kid right out of college. I loved the adrenaline rush and uncertainty of breaking news, the camaraderie and friendships made over the years; I loved knowing things first, then telling others and seeing their reaction. Nothing was better than helping police catch a criminal or when a story in a newscast helped a member of the community right an injustice.

But after seven years, I got antsy and was ready for the taste of a bigger market, a bigger city and a bigger paycheck. I landed a job in Seattle and moved my family. I quickly moved up the producing ranks in Seattle and in five years, I became the producer of one of the main weekday evening newscasts. At age 30, I was also the youngest producer at the time. My life was perfect; I was living my dream and I was on top of the world. Then it came to a crashing end when my boss, who had promoted me three times in three years, left the station a couple of years later. She was replaced by someone who ultimately wanted his own people and I was soon demoted.

I felt humiliated and defeated. I would have loved nothing more than to tell my new boss to shove it, but I was trapped. I had one basket. My job was my only source of income. I sank into a low and a depression I had never experienced before. In addition, my physical health started to suffer. There was always an excuse not to go to the gym; I began to eat poorly, became a couch potato and was tired all the time. I just wanted to crawl into a hole and stay there. Even my son noticed and asked why I was spending so much time watching TV. It was embarrassing.

I don't know if it was merely the passage of time that snapped me out of my funk, which lasted several months, or that I simply realized I couldn't continue that way. I was tired of wandering aimlessly and tired of being tired. I had abandoned reading for months, so I started again, to reconnect with positive thoughts and feelings. I set out to find another job where my talent and experience would be appreciated. I was also looking for another stream of income; one that would finally give me that financial freedom I was seeking.

I used to wish I hadn't spent nearly two decades on the career track to realize what I really wanted in life. I still fantasize about traveling back in time and visiting my younger, 20-year-old self. I'm not sure I would have listened to me, but I would have planted the seed that concepts such as residual income and financial freedom existed. And they weren't merely concepts. It was and IS possible if you want it badly enough and you're willing to do what it takes to succeed.

That's the purpose of this book. To catch you in your late teens, twenties or early thirties, so you can begin your path to being Free at 40. So what if you're already 40 or past 40? It is never too late for you. Remember the story of Colonel Sanders of Kentucky Fried Chicken fame. Unable to live on his pension at age 65, he set out to sell his chicken recipe. After 1,008 rejections from restaurant owners, number 1,009 said "yes." And the rest, as you know, is history.

Start dreaming about what you would do with your life if money were no concern. Think back to the time when you were a child and anything was possible. You wanted to be an astronaut, an actor, president, a magician. Nothing was silly or unrealistic. Then somewhere along the way, someone, no matter how well-meaning, told you to "grow up." To get your head out of the clouds. If you're living your dream life, I applaud you. You are an inspiration and shining example to all. If you've lost sight of your dreams, get in touch with your inner child and find what you're truly passionate about. If you have children, you have a duty to teach them to pursue their dreams, not crush them. You have an obligation as a parent to set a good example and live your dream, so your children can see that it's possible.

I encourage you to put together a Dream Board. This is similar to writing down your goals, but it's more visual and there's more of an emotional attachment. Get a piece of poster paper. Put on it photos, pictures, images that inspire you or of things you want or want to do, places you want to go, etc. Nothing is out of reach. Mine includes lots of beach photos (who doesn't like the beach?), a hammock on the beach, a family on the beach, a woman doing yoga on a beach, a woman with a fruity drink sunning on the beach, a beachfront villa in Bora Bora, a private jet, a convertible, a photo of someone driving in a convertible down the Pacific Coast Highway, ballroom dancers in Vienna, sunning on the deck of a boat, fresh, delicious food, a house on a lake… you get the idea.

Once you're done, put it someplace where you'll see it every day. It will serve as a reminder of what you want and where you're going, and serve as inspiration when you're down. In time you'll be amazed, as I was, to watch your dreams come true. Put yourself "out there." You must let it be known what it is you want. God, the Universe, Mother Nature, or whatever higher power you believe in, will provide.

Don't forget that there is work involved. Dreaming without action is merely wishing. Take action and set goals to fulfill your dream. One goal at a time, one step at a time.

A word of caution: be careful who you share your dreams with. Choose your friends wisely. There are people who will tell you that it's all a load of crap. They will ridicule you. They will try to drag you down. Misery loves company. These Dream Killers likely afraid that they will lose you when you do succeed. They have given up on their own dreams and resent you for reminding them of it. You may have to end those friendships if they won't support you. A Dream Killer could also turn out to be a family member. If so, limit the time and interaction you have with this family member.

Where will your dreams take you?

CHAPTER 7 RECAP: (RE)DISCOVER YOUR PASSION AND TAKE ACTION TO LIVE YOUR DREAM.

CHAPTER 8
LESSONS FROM
DAVE RAMSEY

Throughout this book, Robert Kiyosaki is mentioned a number of times. He's a best-selling author with strong opinions about good debt and bad debt. Now I want to highlight a different, some say opposing, school of thought.

Throughout my journey towards financial freedom, I listened daily to this guy on the radio, Dave Ramsey. I found it by accident, but I believe I was meant to find it.

"When the student is ready, the teacher will appear." ~ ancient Buddhist proverb

One day, while driving home from work, I hit the "seek" button on my AM radio and it landed on the Dave Ramsey Show. Dave was telling a caller to sell his car. The caller, who was trying to get out of debt, owed more on the car than it was worth, and Ramsey told him to sell it anyway, and take a note for the difference. Being $4,000 in debt is better than being $18,000 in debt, he argued. I loved how Dave said it was "stoopid" to own a car that's worth more than half of your income. I was hooked. This guy was a breath of fresh air and made a lot of sense.

Dave Ramsey teaches 7 Baby Steps to become debt free. His "Total Money Makeover" book is on my recommended reading list (at the end of this book). The biggest hurdle for most people is Baby Step 2, the "debt snowball," where you pay off your debt, smallest to largest. Debt equals risk, says Ramsey.

The concept of debt was completely foreign to me when I first came to the United States. In college, I often wondered how other students were able to afford nice cars. I lived close to campus and walked to school. Or I got rides from friends who had cars. I didn't attend a private college; it was a public, state university so it was safe to assume that not everyone was wealthy. But it seemed that everyone drove a nice, new car. After I graduated and started working in my first job making minimum wage, I was baffled when a co-worker was able to buy a brand new car after hers was totaled in a wreck. She graduated the same year as me and I knew she was making minimum wage as well. Maybe she comes from a wealthy family, I thought. Then I learned about this thing called "car payments."

I had bought my first car, a 1979 MG convertible, with cash. I loved it and had picked it over a more sensible car. I had a glorious time for several months. Then it started to break down and spend more and more time in the auto repair shop than it did on the road. I was sick of shelling out hundreds of dollars in repairs every few months. Upon moving to Seattle, a city notorious for having rainy weather year-round, and having a new baby, I decided to give up my beloved MG. I was seduced into buying a new car and fell into the trap of making car payments. Soon after that, I added credit card payments to my monthly obligations, then years later, a mortgage payment. It became a vicious cycle and I was stuck when I really wanted out of my job. Getting into debt means you are relinquishing control. You become "slave to the lender," if you're biblically inclined.

Robert Kiyosaki teaches the difference between good debt and bad debt. But I'm with Dave Ramsey on this one. All debt is bad because it adds risk. I want my life as risk-free as possible. I also prefer Dave's plan because it works in good times *and* in bad.

If I could do it all over again, I would avoid debt like the plague. It will slow down your journey to financial freedom.

Dave reminded me the importance of a budget. I've always had one. It just made sense to me to keep track of money in and money out. Financial freedom will never come to you if don't learn to live on less than you make; it doesn't matter if you make $40,000 or $4 million. If you spend it all, you're still broke. What I didn't realize until Dave said it was... if you're making payments on something like a car, it means you couldn't afford it in the first place. The only thing Dave doesn't frown on is a mortgage but it must be a 15-year fixed and no more than a fourth of your take home, not gross, pay.

Another big lesson I learned from Dave is don't play the lottery! I never did anyway, but I was surprised and amused when I first listened to his rant (love his rants) on playing the lotto. In his "other people" voice, he says: "Well Dave, you can't win if you don't play." "Well Dave, someone has to win."

On DaveRamsey.com, he writes:

"Gambling is a tax on the poor and people who can't do math. Don't get mad at me for saying that. This is not a moral position; it is a mathematical, statistical fact. Studies show that the ZIP codes that spend four times what anyone else does on lottery tickets are those in lower-income parts of town."

Listen to Dave and his lively rants on www.daveramsey.com/radio/home. It's not only educational and life-changing, but highly entertaining.

On a more serious note, the most important lesson I learned from Dave was to get term-life insurance. My husband and I got it after years of thinking our employers' plans were sufficient. They weren't. Even if they are, you lose that when you lose or leave your job. And remember that job security is a myth. Once again, this is about taking control and taking responsibility for your family.

To quote finance guru, Suze Orman:

"It is not okay when you get sick, or when you die, to leave financial chaos behind you for everyone else to clean up."

The husband of a good friend of mine died very suddenly. They have two young children and at the time of his death, my friend was pregnant with their third child. She had also quit her high-paying job the year before to become a full-time mom. Thankfully, her husband had taken responsibility and bought term life insurance. My friend is still able to be a full-time mom, thanks to her husband's planning.

You cannot say that you love your family and not have term life insurance. It is inexpensive (likely a lot less than your cell phone bill if you're in good health) and there is no excuse not to get it. You're irresponsible if you don't. Plain and simple. Take care of your own family. Don't hinder their chances of financial freedom by your selfish actions.

CHAPTER 8 RECAP: ELIMINATE RISK FROM YOUR LIFE BY BECOMING COMPLETELY DEBT FREE.

CHAPTER 9
A NEW DIRECTION

Dave Ramsey often talks about authors he likes and recommends good books to read. Driving home one day, I finally decided to look into a book he had mentioned several times in the past. He was recommending it once again to a caller who was stuck in his career: *48 Days to The Work You Love* by Dan Miller.

I found the book in the library and devoured it in one afternoon. Miller mentioned the possibility of doing work you love that gives you passive, residual income... he called it SWISS dollars (Sales While I Sleep Soundly). I was still in a job, earning a small amount of residual income, but nowhere close to financial freedom. So I investigated "48 Days" online. I was frustrated with the way my life was going. I was in a job that no longer fulfilled me; I felt as though I was wandering aimlessly, without a purpose. There has to be more to life than this, I thought. Simply existing wasn't enough for me anymore.

On "48 Days" online, I found that I could connect with a coach who would help me figure all that stuff out and help me learn what I'm meant to do with my life. I filled out a questionnaire and soon Rob and I were talking on the phone, and I decided career/life coaching was what I needed. I felt excited and nervous at the same time. Excited about what lay ahead and discoveries we would make. But I was nervous about "facing my demons." I wasn't sure what those were and what was holding me back from obtaining the success I wanted.

My first coaching session with Rob was a two-hour long conversation where he delved into all aspects of my personal life: family, job, finances, and mental, spiritual, physical health. As you're probably aware, all parts of your life influence one another. You may be able to neglect one part of it for short period of time, but if you ignore it for too long, it will end up hurting the other parts of your life. For example, if you ignore your physical health by eating poorly and not exercising, it will eventually eat away at your personal life, your relationships and even your finances.

Rob had me fill out a series of questions that would help determine my personality. We all know who we are deep down, but it's still very eye-opening to see how we may be perceived by others in the world around us. Ultimately, what I've learned from Rob is to be authentic. Be true to yourself. Yes, I know, it sounds so simple. But not easy.

For two months, Rob and I would chat on the phone (we live in different states) weekly. For two months, we explored the different paths that I might pursue, that aligned with my interests and strengths. One of the possibilities was dancing. I've always loved dancing. I am naturally blessed with a good sense of rhythm and was told at an early age that I was a good dancer. We brainstormed ways to monetize that talent. But it just didn't click.

I wasn't sure when I would have my breakthrough moment, and then it happened. And it was anticlimactic for me. I was expecting a big epiphany; for the clouds to part, the sun the shine through and angels to start singing. But the "discovery" was something I was already familiar with and something I was already doing for a living. Writing. I decided that I would write this book. Writing has always been easy for me. English Composition was my favorite subject in elementary school. It continued in high school where I wrote for my school newspaper and wrote letters to pen pals around the world (for you youngsters, that was before the Internet and Facebook). I pursued and graduated with a degree in journalism, again, because it has always been easy for me. For seventeen years, I worked in the broadcast journalism industry, getting paid very well to do something that was so easy.

Writing about financial freedom seemed like a match made in heaven. I've been passionate about it ever since I first learned about it, but being an introvert, I never had to the courage to articulate it to others. Now I am writing with purpose and, I hope, planting the seed that financial freedom isn't a pipe dream. Rob kept me accountable every step of the way, making sure I finished this book in the time frame I said I would.

Throughout the course of writing this book, I have met so many incredible people; I am amazed every day as to how the universe truly does provide, once you let your dreams be known.

CHAPTER 9 RECAP: LIVE YOUR LIFE WITH PURPOSE. IF YOU DON'T KNOW WHERE YOU'RE GOING, ASK FOR DIRECTIONS.

ROB CLINTON is the founder of 180 Career Coaching. He is a motivated visionary who specializes in guiding people who have a desire or need to move toward that next level in their life and career. He has a deep heart for inspiring people to fully live their lives.

Rob is a member of the 48 Days Coaching Connection at www.48days.net, and endorsed by Dan Miller, author of *48 Days To The Work You Love*. Connect with Rob at www.180coach.com.

CHAPTER 10
THE POWER OF
WORDS

When I was looking for my first non-broadcast job, I looked in the public relations and marketing fields, I also looked at web producer jobs, positions where I felt my writing and communications skills would transfer. I became frustrated when I would get passed over for either being over-qualified or for not having "relevant" experience. Public relations agencies told me I did not have "agency experience." Hiring managers for web producer jobs rejected me because I didn't have online experience. I began whining to my husband saying, "Nobody wants to hire me." He would give me a hug and tell me that wasn't true. After saying "nobody wants to hire me" a few more times, my husband looked at me and said, "Not if you keep talking that way."

That stopped me in my tracks. He was right. He reminded me of the power of words, especially of the ones you say out loud. The universe provides but it also "hears." Putting negative stuff "out there" will work against you, not for you. I stopped those negative words immediately and soon after, I got a phone call from an organization where I had applied a month prior. It was a job I really wanted. It was close to home and I felt like I could finally do some good instead of writing yet another news story on a kidnapping, rape or murder.

Much like changing your mindset and your paradigm (Chapter 5), you must change the words that come out of your mouth. Self-defeating words have a way of coming true. My friend, Juli, caught me a few times as I called myself "an idiot" out loud. She told me to stop and pointed out that I would never let someone else talk to me that way.

I'm sure you've done it, or know someone who does. We're all human. It happens. But you must be mindful of what you say. If you're thinking something negative, change that thought immediately. And catch yourself before you speak it. Yes, it takes time. It's a process, a journey. It's how we grow. Just as you can change your mindset, you can also change what you say. Since this is a book about money, I urge you never to say "I don't care about money," or "money doesn't matter." Money absolutely matters! It's not ALL that matters, but it matters, so never say those things because money will never stay with you for long.

Consider some words or phrases that seem positive but really are negative. One popular phrase is "give back." It's often uttered by people who are successful and want to help a community or person who has helped them. But think about what it implies. It implies that you took something that didn't belong to you. Doesn't "pay it forward" sound so much better? The essence of the phrase does not change but the negativity goes away.

Here's another one that really annoys me and you'll notice it when you file those tax returns every year: "unearned income." It's basically any source of income aside from a job, like income from a rental property or interest and dividends from stocks. I most certainly earned that income since I took a risk on that rental property, stock or whatever. I most definitely earned that money. If you noticed, most "unearned income" is what I refer to throughout this book as passive or residual income. Just the phrase alone, "unearned income," makes you think something nefarious is going on.

One more: "non-profit." Credit to Juli for this one. I never realized this till she pointed it out. Is there something wrong with being for-profit? Does it make you a bad person/company if you're not nonprofit?

This feeds into the poverty mentality of "it's evil to want more." No, it is not. You should be grateful for what you have AND strive to have more. There's nothing wrong with having more or wanting more.

In his book *The Science of Getting Rich*, Wallace Wattles said it best:

"It is perfectly right that you should give your best

attention to the Science of Getting Rich, for it is the noblest and most necessary of all studies. If you neglect this study, you are derelict in your duty to yourself, to God and humanity; for you can render to God and humanity no greater service than to make the most of yourself."

CHAPTER 10 RECAP: BE CAREFUL WHAT YOU SAY OUT LOUD. THE UNIVERSE "HEARS" YOU AND WILL PROVIDE WHAT YOU UTTER.

CHAPTER 11
ANOTHER SUCCESS
STORY

"We are living in a time when so many possibilities exist that didn't before."

That's what struck me most about what Kathleen said, as I interviewed her for this book. I first mentioned Kathleen briefly in Chapter 4, as the friend of Juli's who introduced her to the world of network marketing.

Kathleen spent over twenty years in the corporate world and another four more years as a top producing real estate agent. But she really wanted to become a full time investor and take control of her own financial future after reading Robert Kiyosaki's book, *Rich Dad, Poor Dad.*

When she first started investing, Kathleen put her money in individual stocks, then real estate. At the same time, she started investing in herself by attending wealth building seminars. At one of those seminars, participants were asked to share what they were grateful for. Kathleen revealed that she was grateful for her mindset. I asked why that was so important and she said that you can't do anything without a belief system in place.

It was Henry Ford who said:

"Whether you think you can, or you think you can't-- you're right."

I wrote extensively about mindset and shifting your paradigm in Chapter 5. I discussed this with Kathleen and we both agreed that 80 percent of the battle is in your mind. (I love it when a millionaire agrees with me!) Once you believe, the rest of the 20 percent will come more easily. You've seen throughout this book the influence various books have had on the lives of people I've highlighted. Books contain new ideas which stretch your mind and if you choose (yes, once again, it is a choice), change your mindset. Kathleen reminded me of the quote by Charlie Jones:

"You are the same today as you'll be five years from now, except for two things: the people you meet and the books you read."

Kathleen urges you to read books consistently, even if it's just for fifteen minutes a day and be careful who you associate with. With the millionaire mindset, books and a core group of like-minded people, Kathleen was able to achieve financial freedom within ten years after she "got the entrepreneurial bug."

At the beginning of this chapter, Kathleen talked about the endless possibilities. It's due in part to the advances in technology and the Internet. With very little or no money, you can make a lot by selling a product online. Starting up a business does not require a ton of capital, investors, employees or any overhead. And the Internet is just one avenue where you can build or create a passive, residual income stream.

Kathleen urges women to "find your voice" while you're young. Read all you can about financial literacy and find your passion. If you have a job, invest at least 15 percent of your income. Kathleen says your job will pay your bills. But it's what you do during your off-time that will create long-time wealth. If you have children, teach them at a young age to control their money. Or it will end up controlling them.

Kathleen is helping to raise two young girls and a boy with her partner and they are teaching them to put their allowance in four different jars: saving, investing, spending and giving. Recently, each of the children invested $200 into a stock, which they have been encouraged to track online. We should all have "jars" of money. There are too many people who spend all they make, and then some (credit card debt). Then they wake up one day and wonder, "where did all my money go?" Control your money and you will have better control of your life.

Kathleen's not only helping kids close to her. She is the co-founder of Estrellas Para Ninos, which builds orphanages for children in Juarez, Mexico. It has now expanded to Rwanda and Cambodia. There are a total of 14 homes for kids who would otherwise live on the streets and be subjected to kidnapping, rape, even murder. Once you take care of yourself and the needs of your loved ones, then you can begin to make a difference in the world. Kathleen says that is the best part and also when the fun begins.

Kathleen became financially free in her mid to late 40's. You can do it too.

CHAPTER 11 RECAP: TAKE IT FROM A MILLIONAIRE: READ BOOKS CONSISTENTLY, BE CAREFUL WHO YOU ASSOCIATE WITH.

KATHLEEN DEGGELMAN enjoys the success of her business today because she followed her passions for food, travel and financial empowerment. Kathleen is now living her dream: traveling the world and helping people create financial freedom and wealth with a multi-patented health and nutrition company. Kathleen is also a professional speaker and is available to speak to audiences about health and nutrition, as well as building a business. Connect with Kathleen at www.KathleenDeggelman.com or www.FreeGiftFromKathleen.com.

CHAPTER 12
PAY NOW OR PAY LATER

Throughout this book, I've talked about choices. Ultimately, we all decide whether to pay the price now, or pay it later. This applies to all aspects of your life, not just money.

In matters of physical health, you can make the choice daily to exercise your body so it stays in prime form. It is a price of thirty minutes a day for five days a week, or 150 minutes a week. If you don't pay this price now, while you're young, you will pay the price later. I saw this price paid firsthand by my own father. Years of a sedentary lifestyle took its toll and he died from heart disease at the age of 52.

A study by Duke University Medical Center shows patients who did not exercise gained approximately four pounds a year. A sedentary lifestyle leads to increases in visceral fat, which accumulates around the organs inside the belly. A lack of exercise leads to so-called "lifestyle diseases"… cancer, high blood pressure, high cholesterol, obesity, low back pain, many more.

Along with exercise is the importance of a good diet. Again, this is a daily choice. A 2004 study published in the Journal of Food Composition and Analysis reveals Americans are getting nearly a third of their calories from junk foods: sweets, desserts, salty snacks; foods filled with empty calories with little or no nutritional value. Pay now by making good diet choices every day. Or pay later with poor health and higher insurance premiums and medical bills that can bankrupt you and your family.

How are you choosing to spend evenings after work? Do you prop yourself in front of the television and turn into a zombie? Or do you choose to use that time to soak in knowledge that will feed your mind with positive and productive ideas? There is nothing wrong with the occasional indulgence of mindless entertainment. But like indulging too much in fatty food, it will turn your mind to mush.

What does the mind and body have to do with wealth? Everything. What good is wealth if you do not have the state of mind and good health to enjoy it? Make the choice to do good things for your mind, body and spirit today and every day. Small increments over time, much like compound interest in your 401(k), lead to great results. Better to pay little increments now than a big "balloon" payment that could destroy you later.

Rome was not built in a day; wealth cannot be built overnight. Yes, you could win the lottery. But the majority of lottery winners lose it all in a few years.

It's because they never developed the proper habits to stay wealthy. It's very much like going on a fad diet. You could lose a lot of weight in a short amount of time, then gain it all back and more. It's because you never developed the daily habits needed to maintain a healthy weight.

Pay now or pay later. Either way, you pay. Now that you've reached the end of this book, I hope you will continue on your journey towards financial freedom. Look into all the great books and authors who have helped me and feel free to share any I may have missed on the public forum of my web site www.Freeat40.com.

CHAPTER 12 RECAP: MAKE GOOD CHOICES DAILY IN YOUR MENTAL, PHYSICAL, SPIRITUAL AND FINANCIAL HEALTH.

ABOUT ME

As of this writing, I am 21 months away from my 40th birthday and still on the journey to financial freedom. I recently switched careers and took a significant pay cut. I am earning a residual income from my network marketing business but not enough just yet to cover my living expenses. Just like many of you, I have my struggles and challenges with money. But I strongly believe financial freedom is near. I welcome your stories and thoughts at www.freeat40.com; that's also where you can keep up to date on my journey.

My next book, Fit at 40, is expected to be released in December 2011. As the title implies, it is about staying fit at age 40 and beyond. It will include the stories of amazing women I have the privilege of knowing and their habits on maintaining a healthy weight and lifestyle.

RECOMMENDED READING LIST

(to get you started. There are many more books like these out there.)

Think and Grow Rich Napoleon Hill
The Science of Getting Rich Wallace Wattles
The Total Money Makeover Dave Ramsey
Rich Dad, Poor Dad Robert Kiyosaki
Cash Flow Quadrant Robert Kiyosaki
How To Win Friends and Influence People Dale Carnegie
Women & Money Suze Orman
The 9 Steps to Financial Freedom Suze Orman
The Money Class Suze Orman
The Millionaire Next Door Thomas Stanley, William Danko
Secrets of the Millionaire Mind T. Harv Eker
48 Days To The Work You Love Dan Miller
No More Mondays Dan Miller
The 4-Hour Workweek Timothy Ferriss
Fired To Hired Tory Johnson
The 7 Habits of Highly Effective People Stephen Covey
Good To Great Jim Collins
Tribes Seth Godin
Purple Cow Seth Godin
Eat That Frog Brian Tracy
The One Minute Millionaire Robert Allen & Mark Victor Hansen